my very first joke book

KAYE UMANSKY

Illustrated by Ian Cunliffe

PUFFIN

I SAY, I SAY, I SAY...

Who led ten thousand pigs up the hill and back down again?

The Grand Old Duke of Pork.

1

Why did Cinderella sleep in the fireplace?

She always slept like a log.

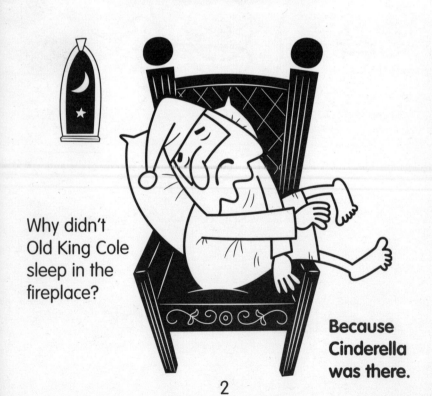

Why didn't
Old King Cole
sleep in the
fireplace?

**Because
Cinderella
was there.**

Why was Cinderella no good at football?

She ran away from the ball.

How did the sheep feel when Bo Peep lost them?

Baaaa-aaaaad.
Real baaa-aaaaaad.

Who shouted "knickers!" at the Big Bad Wolf?

Little **Rude** Riding Hood.

What's the hardest thing about learning to ride a bike?

The ground.

Why couldn't the biscuit find its way home?

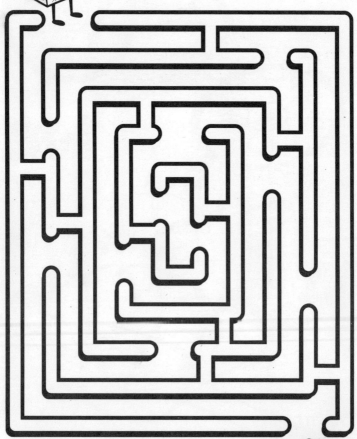

It had been a **wafer** too long.

What's the difference between a penguin and a biscuit?

You can't dunk a penguin in a glass of milk.

How do you know

which end of the worm

is its head?

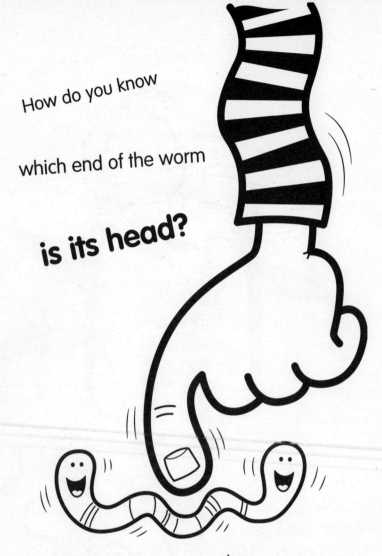

Tickle its tummy and see which end giggles.

What do you call a duck with a big ice cream?

A lucky ducky.

If he gets it all over him, he's a mucky ducky.

How do you make an apple crumble?

Hit it with a hammer.

What's covered in custard and complains?

Rhubarb grumble.

What do you call a gorilla with two bananas in his ears?

Hey, smelly!

Anything you like, because he can't hear you.

What kind of noise annoys an oyster?

A noisy noise annoys an oyster most.

(Now say it fast!)

Why did the lobster blush?

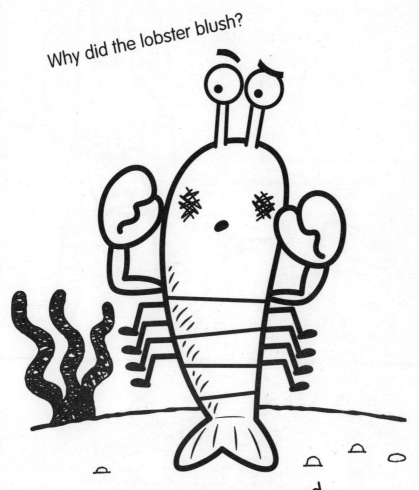

Because the sea weed.

18

How do you know when there's
an elephant hiding under your bed?

Your nose touches the ceiling.

Why did Humpty Dumpty go into the jungle?

He was an **egg**-splorer.

OVERHEARD

Two eggs were in a saucepan.
One said, "Phew! I'm boiling!"
The other said, "Wait till you get out,
you'll get your head bashed in."

Man in pet shop:
"Got any dogs going cheap?"

Owner:
"No. All ours go
'WOOF'."

Cat owner:
"Our cat's swallowed
a ball of wool."

Vet:
"Congratulations, sir!
She'll soon be
having mittens."

"Waiter, waiter! Will my pancake be **long**?"

"No. Round."

"Blame the chicken – I only laid the table."

"Waiter, waiter! Bring me
a crocodile sandwich,

and make it snappy!"

Man: "How long will this bus be?"

Woman: "The same length as the last one."

28

30

DOCTORS & DENTISTS

"Doctor, Doctor, my tongue is as yellow as custard, and my legs are as wobbly as jelly."

"You're a trifle ill."

"Doctor, Doctor, I think I'm a bumblebee."

"Doctor, Doctor, I think I'm an octopus!"

"Don't worry, I can help you."

"Really? Or are you just pulling my

leg, leg, leg, leg, leg, leg, leg, leg?"

"Pull yourself together."

"Doctor, Doctor, I think I'm the Invisible Man."

"Who said that?"

What time do you go to the dentist?

Tooth hurty.

Dentist: "I haven't touched your tooth yet. Why are you screaming?"

Patient: "Because you are standing on my foot."

"Doctor, Doctor, my hair's falling out. Can you give me something to keep it in?"

"Certainly. Here's a paper bag."

KNOCK, KNOCK

"Knock, knock."
"Who's there?"
"Justin."
"Justin who?"
"Justin time for dinner."

41

"Knock, knock."
"Who's there?"
"Lucy."
"Lucy who?"

"Lucy Lastic! Your pants are falling down!"

"Knock, knock."

"Who's there?"

"Panther."

"Panther who?"

"Panther no panths, I'm going thwimming."

44

"**Knock, knock.**"   "Who's there?"   "**Cowsgo.**"

"Cowsgo who?"   "**No. Cows go, 'moo'.**"

45

"Knock, knock."
"Who's there?"
Hammond.
"Hammond who?"
"Hammond Eggs."

MONSTERS

What does a monster eat after all his teeth have been pulled out?

The dentist.

48

49

What does a monster eat for lunch?

Boiled legs and soldiers.

What did the policeman say to the three-headed monster?

What do you call
a monster with
seven ears?

Eerie.

And one with
seven noses?

Nosey.

And one with
seven hands?

Andy.

CROSS-BREEDS

What do you get if you cross . . .

A sheep with a kangaroo?

A woolly jumper.

A cow with a duck?

Cream quackers.

53

What do you get if you cross . . .

A cockerel with a poodle?

A cockerpoodledoo.

Baaa

A baby goat with white chocolate?

The milky-baa kid.

54

SILLY RHYMES

Jack Sprat could eat no fat,

His wife could eat no lean.

They lived on peas and broccoli,

And now they've both turned green.

Mary had a little bull,
She kept it as a pet.

It tossed poor Mary down the well, And now she's soaking wet!

57

Sing a song of sixpence,
A pocketful of rye.
Four-and-twenty blackbirds
Pecked me in the eye!

JOKE LIBRARY

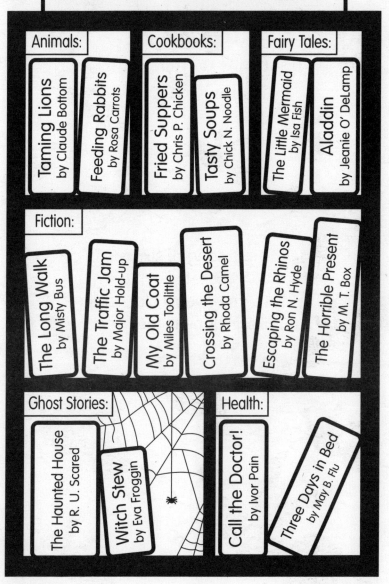

Animals:
- Taming Lions by Claude Bottom
- Feeding Rabbits by Rosa Carrots

Cookbooks:
- Fried Suppers by Chris P. Chicken
- Tasty Soups by Chick N. Noodle

Fairy Tales:
- The Little Mermaid by Isa Fish
- Aladdin by Jeanie O' DeLamp

Fiction:
- The Long Walk by Misty Bus
- The Traffic Jam by Major Hold-up
- My Old Coat by Miles Toolittle
- Crossing the Desert by Rhoda Camel
- Escaping the Rhinos by Ron N. Hyde
- The Horrible Present by M. T. Box

Ghost Stories:
- The Haunted House by R. U. Scared
- Witch Stew by Eva Froggin

Health:
- Call the Doctor! by Ivor Pain
- Three Days in Bed by May B. Flu